Date: 6/15/16

KENYA

by Sherra G. Edgar

The Child's World®

Published by The Child's World®
1980 Lookout Drive • Mankato, MN 56003-1705
800-599-READ • www.childsworld.com

Acknowledgments
The Child's World®: Mary Berendes, Publishing Director
Red Line Editorial: Editorial direction
The Design Lab: Design
Amnet: Production

Design elements: Shutterstock Images; iStock/Thinkstock; A. Jaredwell/Shutterstock Images; Solodov Alexey/Shutterstock Images
Photographs ©: Shutterstock Images, cover (left top), cover (right), 1 (top), 5, 16, 18 (right), 21, 24, 25; iStock/Thinkstock, cover (left, middle top), 1 (bottom left, top), 18 (left top); A. Jaredwell/Shutterstock Images, cover (left, middle bottom), 1 (bottom left, bottom), 18 (left bottom); Solodov Alexey/Shutterstock Images, cover (left bottom), 1 (bottom right); Jonathan Pledger/Shutterstock Images, 6–7; John Wollwerth/Shutterstock Images, 8; W. L. Davies/iStockphoto, 10, 12; Byelikova Oksana/iStockphoto, 11; iStockphoto, 13; Byelikova Oksana/Shutterstock Images, 14, 30; Andrzej Grzegorczyk/Shutterstock Images, 17; Marja Schwartz/iStockphoto, 20; Britta Kasholm-Tengve/iStockphoto, 22, 27, 28

ISBN 9781634070522
LCCN 2014922471

Printed in the United States of America
Mankato, MN
July, 2015
PA02268

ABOUT THE AUTHOR
Sherra G. Edgar lives in Lumberton, Texas. She has taught primary school for 19 years and has written many books for children. Edgar enjoys spending time with family and friends, reading, and watching movies.

ONE WORLD • MANY COUNTRIES •

TABLE OF CONTENTS

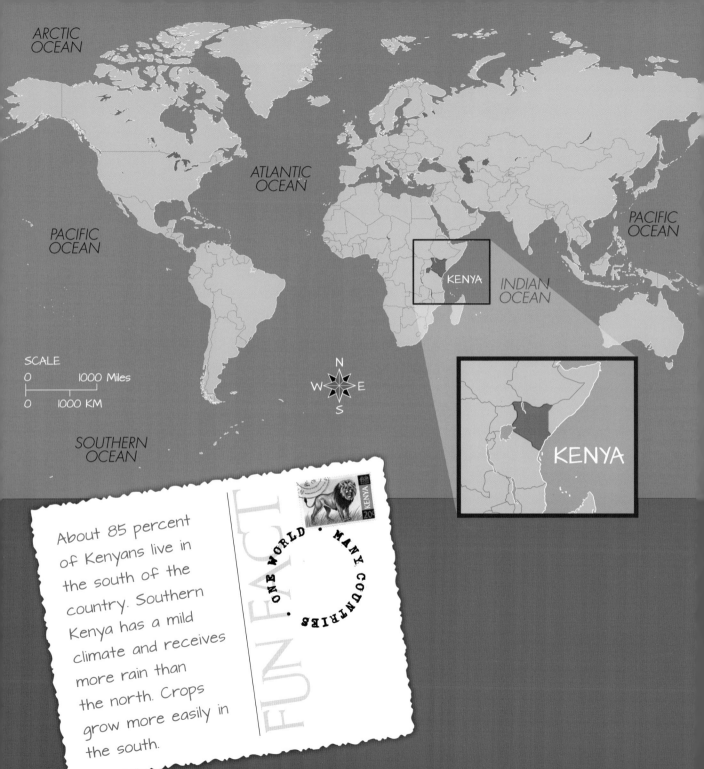

ARCTIC
OCEAN

ATLANTIC
OCEAN

PACIFIC
OCEAN

PACIFIC
OCEAN

KENYA

INDIAN
OCEAN

SCALE

0   1000 Miles

0   1000 KM

SOUTHERN
OCEAN

N
W E
S

KENYA

About 85 percent
of Kenyans live in
the south of the
country. Southern
Kenya has a mild
climate and receives
more rain than
the north. Crops
grow more easily in
the south.

FUN FACT

ONE WORLD · MANY COUNTRIES

KENYA 20¢

CHAPTER 1

WELCOME TO KENYA!

It is a cool night in Mombasa, Kenya's second-largest city. Music fills the air. People sing and dance. They enjoy a bowl of *ugali*, one of Kenya's national dishes.

Children stretch their necks to spy the first float of the parade. The music swells while colorful floats move down the streets. The children laugh and wave. They point as their favorite floats go by. This is the Mombasa Carnival.

Kenya is home to almost 45 million people.

This festival celebrates Kenya's great **diversity**. Kenya is a large country in Africa. It is home to more than 70 **ethnic** groups and more than 40 tribes. Some people live in large cities. Others live in tiny villages.

Kenya is a favorite **safari** destination. Lions, leopards, elephants, and rhinos all live in Kenya. The land is the perfect home for these animals. Scientists come from all over the world to study them.

Elephants and other animals are protected in Kenya's more than 50 wildlife reserves.

CHAPTER 2

THE LAND

Mount Kenya is the second-tallest peak in Africa. It is 17,076 feet (5,205 m) tall.

Kenya is in eastern Africa. Ethiopia borders Kenya to the north. Somalia and the Indian Ocean border Kenya to the east. Uganda is Kenya's western neighbor. The Indian Ocean and Tanzania form Kenya's southern border.

Kenya's land sits on a **rift**. Mount Kenya is on the western side of the rift. Mount Elgon is on the rift's eastern side. Mount Elgon is on the border between Kenya and Uganda. Both mountains are inactive volcanoes.

The sun rises over the Great Rift Valley.

Below the mountains are valleys. The Great Rift Valley has deserts. These desert areas run into northern Kenya. The Great Rift Valley is also where Lake Turkana is located. Lake Turkana is the lowest point on the valley floor.

Kenya's climate varies across the country. In the mountains, it gets very cold. The mountains are often capped with snow.

Lake Turkana's waters are rich in fish, crocodiles, and hippopotamuses.

In the deserts, it is hot and dry during the day and cool at night. Along the coast, the climate is wetter and warmer. This is because it is located near the Indian Ocean.

Kenya has many natural resources. One of the most important is limestone. Most of Kenya's limestone comes from the Indian Ocean. Limestone is used to make cement. Cement production is one of Kenya's largest industries.

Another one of Kenya's great natural resources is its wildlife. Many people come from all over the world to see Kenya's animals. They take safaris, which allow visitors to observe

On safaris, people ride in vehicles that take them close to wild animals.

animals in the wild. People enjoy seeing elephants, lions, and crocodiles in their natural homes. Safaris make up a large part of Kenya's **tourism**.

FUN FACT

The Masai Mara National Reserve is in the Great Rift Valley. It is a popular place to view Kenya's wildlife. Visitors to the reserve are able to see buffalo, elephants, leopards, lions, and rhinoceroses.

ONE WORLD · MANY COUNTRIES

CHAPTER 3

GOVERNMENT AND CITIES

Citizens in Lamu, Kenya, participate in a political rally.

Kenya's official name is the **Republic** of Kenya. Citizens vote for their leaders. The highest leader in Kenya is the president. The president works with advisors and lawmakers. They work together to make decisions for the country.

Kenya has eight **provinces**. They are similar to states. Each province has a local leader.

Kenya's largest city is Nairobi. Nairobi is the capital of Kenya. It is in central Kenya. Nairobi is Kenya's main

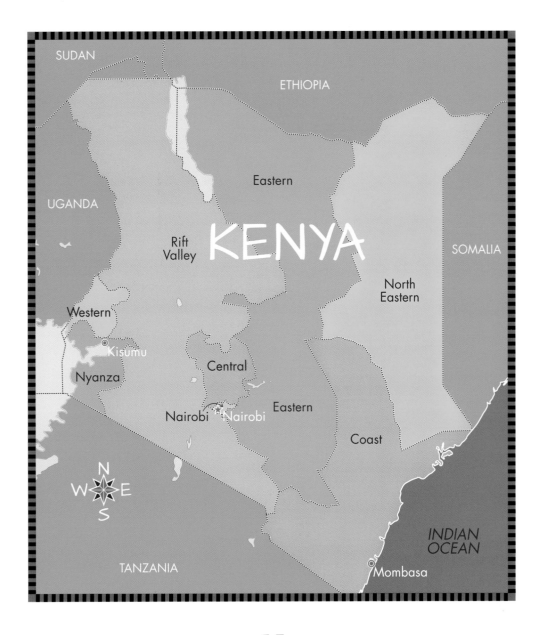

Skyscrapers fill the skyline in Nairobi's business district.

center of industry. Many of the country's businesses have headquarters there.

Mombasa is Kenya's second-largest city. About 1.2 million people live there. Mombasa is an island in the Indian Ocean. It is connected to the mainland by a large freeway. Mombasa has a large port and an international airport.

Mombasa is a popular place for tourists visiting Kenya. The Mombasa Marine National Park and Reserve is an exciting place to visit. Much of Kenya's wildlife is protected in the reserve.

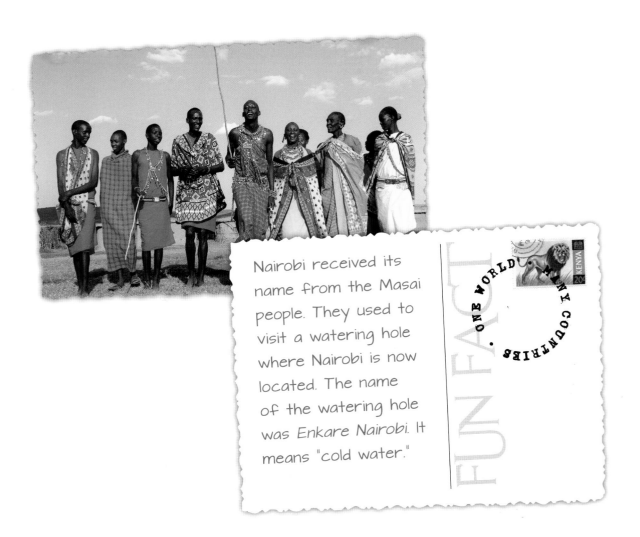

Nairobi received its name from the Masai people. They used to visit a watering hole where Nairobi is now located. The name of the watering hole was Enkare Nairobi. It means "cold water."

Kenya's third largest-city is Kisumu. This city is in western Kenya. It is located on the coast of Lake Victoria. Kisumu has a large port, called Port Florence. It is also the site of the main station for the Ugandan Railway.

Kenya's **economy** is growing. Tourism is one of Africa's biggest industries. Many tourists enjoy safaris in any of Kenya's

19 national parks. Other tourist attractions include the Great Rift Valley and Mombasa **mosques**.

Seventy-five percent of the jobs in Kenya are in farming. Some of the crops grown in Kenya include tea, coffee, sugarcane, wheat, fruits, and vegetables. Kenyans also make farming machinery and parts. The machines and crops are **exported**.

Another industry in Kenya is oil refining. Much of the world's oil is found in Kenya. Refined oil is sold to other countries.

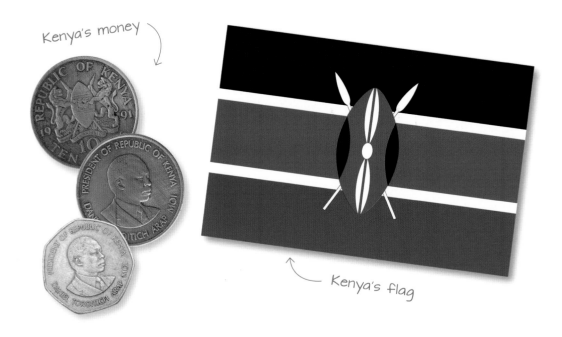

Kenya's money

Kenya's flag

GLOBAL CONNECTIONS

Every year, thousands of people from other African countries move to Kenya. Most of the people who move come from neighboring countries, such as South Sudan, Ethiopia, and Somalia.

The largest group of people who move to Kenya are from Somalia. Somalis want to escape the fighting and violence that have been going on in their country since 1991. They believe that Kenya will provide them a peaceful place to live.

Nearly half a million Somalis have moved to Kenya. They often live in crowded camps where conditions are poor. Kenya does not have enough resources to care for all of the Somalis and others who move to Kenya. For this reason, Kenyan leaders have asked for help from the United Nations.

The United Nations is group of countries that work together. They help people throughout the world. In Kenya, the United Nations is providing basic goods to the Somalis, such as clean water, healthcare, and schools. It also raises money to buy other needed supplies.

CHAPTER 4

PEOPLE AND CULTURES

The people of Kenya are very diverse. Kenya is home to more than 70 ethnic groups. These different groups are united under the Kenyan flag. The people have a saying that describes this process of coming together. It is called *harambee*, which means "let's all pull together."

A man from the Kikuyu tribe wears a traditional mask and face painting.

Kenya's largest ethnic group is the Kikuyu. They form about 20 percent of Kenya's population. The Kikuyu people live near Mount Kenya. For many years they worked as farmers. They grew crops such as peas and beans. Today, many Kikuyu are leaders in Kenya's businesses and government.

The Masai are Kenya's second-largest group. They are **nomads** who live in the Great Rift Valley. Life for the Masai has changed little in hundreds of years. They spend their days searching for water and food for their cattle.

In Masai culture, older children take care of younger ones.

The Swahili are people who live along Kenya's coast. These people are a blend of many groups that have come to Kenya. Swahili people are a mix of Arab, Persian, Portuguese, Omani, and native Kenyan peoples.

More than 80 tribal languages are spoken in Kenya. These tribal languages are an important part of a Kenyan's identity. The country's official languages are Kiswahili and English. Most Kenyans can speak their tribal languages, as well as Kiswahili or English.

Religion is also important to many Kenyans. More than 80 percent of Kenyans are Christian. The coast has a large population of people who practice Islam. Many people also practice traditional tribal beliefs.

Kenya has two important national holidays. Jamhuri Day is celebrated on December 6. It marks Kenya's independence from England in 1963. On June 1, Kenyans celebrate Madaraka Day. It honors the day Kenya become a republic.

A Masai boy learns to read and write at a school in Porini, Kenya.

Kenya is known for its long-distance runners. In 2011, the world's 20 fastest marathon runners were all from Kenya. They have won numerous Olympic medals and international marathons.

FUN FACT

ONE WORLD · MANY COUNTRIES

KENYA 20

CHAPTER 5

DAILY LIFE

Traditional Masai huts are placed close together to form a village.

In Kenya, daily life is different between cities and villages. It is common for cities to be modern and fast-paced. They have restaurants, shops, theaters, and universities. In villages, life has a slower pace. Clothing, food, and homes are very traditional.

In Kenya's cities, people live in high-rise apartments or modern houses. People in villages often live in huts. These huts are made of wood and mud. The roofs are made by weaving branches, leaves, or other plants together.

Kenya does have not one kind of traditional clothing. The country is diverse, so there are many types of dress. Some people in cities wear clothing similar to what is worn in the United States. Some villagers dress in bright colors. These colors represent their tribes. Other Kenyans dress according to their religion. Muslims sometimes wear togas and turbans.

Kenya has many traditional foods. One dish is *ugali*. *Ugali* is cornmeal that is cooked until it is similar to porridge. Then the porridge is baked until it is a dough. It is the most common food in Kenya.

Transportation in Kenya differs according to place. In small villages, people mostly walk. Many villages do not have paved roads. They are often very far into the forests. This makes it difficult for vehicles to reach villages.

In the cities there are cars, buses, and railways. The most common form of transportation in Kenyan cities is by *matatu*. *Matatus* are similar to minivans or mini-buses. They are privately owned. The *matatus* are often decorated with bright colors, pictures, or sayings.

Walking is a common way to get from place to place in Kenya.

As in other parts of the world, family is important to Kenyans. Extended family members often live together. Children are expected to care for their parents as they age.

The sense of pride in family and tribe is important in Kenya. People are also proud of their nation. It has a great diversity of wildlife, landscapes, and people. All the diversity comes together in Kenya to create a unique nation.

In January 2003, Kenya's schools became free. In that first month, 1.3 million new students began attending school.

DAILY LIFE FOR CHILDREN

Daily life for children in Kenya is different from place to place. Some children from wealthy families go to school and play soccer. Their life, in some ways, is like life in the United States.

For other children, life is very different. In Kenya, some children go to work at a very young age. Their families are poor. They need to make more money. Some Kenyan children work in unclean and unsafe environments. Kenyan leaders are trying to pass new laws to protect the country's children.

A popular food in Kenya is nyama choma. Nyama choma means "roasted meat." This meat is usually either beef or goat. The meat is roasted or grilled.

FUN FACT

ONE WORLD • MANY COUNTRIES

KENYA 20¢

FAST FACTS

Population: 45 million

Area: 224,081 square miles (580,367 sq km)

Capital: Nairobi

Largest Cities: Nairobi and Mombasa

Form of Government: Republic

Languages: English and Kiswahili

Trading Partners: Uganda, Tanzania, India, and China

Major Holidays: Jamhuri Day and Madaraka Day

National Dish: *Ugali* (a thick porridge made of cornmeal)

Tourists on a safari in Masai Mara National park take photos of giraffes.

GLOSSARY

diversity (di-VUR-suh-tee) Diversity is the state of having many different people, groups, or types of things. Kenya's people represent a diversity of tribes.

ethnic (ETH-nik) Ethnic describes a group with a common language, culture, religion, or background. Kenya has many ethnic groups.

exported (EK-sported) Exported describes goods that have been sold to another country. Kenya's crops are exported.

mosques (MAHSKS) Mosques are Muslim places of worship. People go to mosques to pray.

nomads (NO-mads) Nomads are people who move from place to place. The Masai are nomads.

provinces (PRAH-vens-ez) Provinces are large areas that some countries are divided into. Kenya has eight provinces.

republic (ree-PUB-lick) A republic is a place where an elected official rules over the land and people. Kenya is a republic.

rift (rift) A rift is a crack in Earth's crust. Kenya's land is situated on a rift.

safari (suh-FAR-ee) A safari is a trip where people look for wild animals. Taking a safari is popular in Kenya.

tourism (TOOR-ih-zum) Tourism is the act of people traveling for pleasure. Tourism is important to Kenya's economy.

TO LEARN MORE

BOOKS

Cunnane, Kelly. *For You Are a Kenyan Child.*
New York: Atheneum Books for Young Readers, 2006.

Giles, Bridget. *Kenya.* Washington, D.C.:
National Geographic, 2006.

Nivola, Claire A. *Planting the Trees of Kenya: The Story of
Wangari Maathai.* New York: Farrar, Straus, and Giroux, 2008.

WEB SITES

Visit our Web site for links about Kenya: **childsworld.com/links**

*Note to Parents, Teachers, and Librarians: We routinely verify our Web links to make
sure they are safe and active sites. So encourage your readers to check them out!*

INDEX